Table of Contents

KT-364-320

Puppy Care and Training

T.F.H. Publications
One TFH Plaza
Third and Union Avenues
Neptune City, NJ 07753

This book has been published with the intent to provide accurate and authoritative information in regard to the subject matter within. While every precaution has been taken in preparation of this book, the publisher and author assume no responsibility for errors or omissions. Neither is any liability assumed for damages resulting from the use of the information herein.

ISBN 0-7938-1000-0

www.tfh.com

Bringing Your Puppy Home

You have done your homework and have chosen your ideal puppy, and now you are probably anxious to get him home. There are a few things that you should do before the puppy steps into your house to ensure that you get off on the right foot. Remember that puppies are just like babies. You wouldn't bring home a new baby before you had a car seat, crib, diapers, clothes, and all the other equipment you'd need to keep the child safe and comfortable. The same holds true for your new canine addition.

Veterinary Care
The first thing you should do is to find a good veterinarian in the

area. Your puppy should visit the veterinarian within 48 to 72 hours of his arrival home to make sure he is healthy and to set up his vaccination schedule. Also, you never know when an emergency may arise, and it is better to be safe than sorry—select your veterinarian before you need him.

You should take your new puppy to the veterinarian within 48 to 72 hours of acquiring him.

When searching for a vet, you can ask your local humane society or animal shelter for vets in the area, ask your dog-owning friends whom they use, or if the puppy's breeder lives in your area, ask her for a recommendation. Once you have the name of a few veterinarians, you should visit each one. Check out the facilities and meet the doctor and his staff. Inspect the office and make sure it is clean, well lit, and sufficiently supervised. Make sure the veterinarian is familiar with your breed of puppy. Ask about his hours, his emergency policies, his payment policies, and his specialties. Once you are comfortable with your choice, you can make an appointment to bring your puppy in a few days after you pick him up.

Supplies

There are certain things that your puppy will need immediately, so it is best if you go out and purchase them before he comes home. The better prepared you are for your puppy's arrival, the smoother the transition will be for everyone.

Things You Need to Buy for the Puppy's Arrival:

- Food and water bowls
- Puppy food
- Collar and leash
- Soft bed or bedding for crate
- Crate
- Baby gates
- Grooming tools
- Toys
- ID Tag

Setting Up a Puppy Care Schedule

Once you have all the basic equipment ready for your puppy, you should map out a tentative schedule with members of your family. Figure out who can be with him and at what times, because he will need constant supervision for the first few days. The worst thing you can do is bring home a new puppy and leave him alone. He will be unsure of his environment, scared, and lonely, and his first impressions will stay with him for a long time. You should think about where the puppy will be kept, where he will eat, where he will sleep, and where he will be taken to eliminate. It is also a good time to take a look around at your existing environment and see if your home is safe enough for your puppy to move into.

Puppy-Proofing Your Home

Your little puppy will be very curious about his new surroundings, and with typical puppy energy, will want to investigate everything

Puppy-Appropriate Toys

Make sure that you buy toys that are the right size for your puppy. Most packages will indicate the size of the dog for which the toy is made. Also, make sure to monitor your dog's chewing, and when the chew toy gets too small or pieces start to break off, take the toy away. This will prevent your puppy from choking on small pieces or swallowing pieces that can get lodged in his stomach or intestines. A great choice for puppies is the Nylabone® Puppy Starter Kit of chews.

that is available to him. The trick is to make the dangerous things unavailable to him by puppy-proofing your home. The best way to do this is to get down on your puppy's level and take a look around. What can he get into? What can he jump up on? What can he open up or chew on? Don't ever assume that your puppy won't touch something, because if he can get into trouble, he will. There are many potential dangers within the home for a little mischievous puppy, so you must think about these in advance and make sure he is protected from them.

If your train your puppy to have good chewing habits, he will have healthy teeth throughout his lifetime.

Quick Tip

Check out these things around your house that may be dangerous to your puppy and keep him away from them or keep them out of his reach:

- Electrical wires
- Open doors
- Balconies
- Medicines
- Soaps and shampoos
- Detergents, household cleansers

- Products for your car, such as antifreeze, motor oil, gasoline
- Outside chemicals such as fertilizer, insecticides, paint, and paint removers
- Plants

Preparing Your Family

If you have children, it is very likely that they will be the most excited when you bring your puppy home. In their enthusiasm, however, children can get carried away and unintentionally hurt or frighten a small puppy. To make sure that the transition goes as smoothly as possible, you must set some ground rules before the puppy arrives. Children should be taught from the outset that a puppy is not a plaything to be dragged around—and they should be promptly scolded if they disobey.

Toddlers and small children should never be left unsupervised with puppies. They must be taught to respect animals and to be gentle with them. If children frighten the puppy at a young age, the feeling might stay with him as he matures. Also, the puppy may nip or scratch in fear, which could harm or scare your children. Mutual regard for one another must be taught from the outset of their relationship. Teach your children that your puppy is a living thing that has feelings and can be hurt, and make sure that the puppy is given a break and allowed to have quiet time away from excited "siblings."

Emergency!

If your dog does eat something he shouldn't, you can call the National Animal Poison Control Center (NAPCC). They have a staff of over 40 licensed vets and board certified toxicologists and can be reached 24 hours a day. Call 1-800-548-2423,and you will be charged $30.00 per case on your credit card, with no charge for follow up calls, or call 1-900-680-0000, and be charged $20.00 for five minutes, plus $2.95 for each additional minute—with no follow up.

Remember that puppies are very much like children. Most likely, your puppy will find your child to be the most exciting person in the house. But puppies, much like children, need limits, and they need to rest often and be allowed to relax. If you teach your puppy and your child to be gentle with and to respect each other, there is no doubt that they will soon become the best of friends.

Coming Home

You've been shopping, your house is ready, your kids are ready, you are ready—it's time to pick up your puppy. If possible, you should arrange to take a few days off or to pick up your puppy on a Friday or a weekend in order to spend as much time as possible helping him get adjusted. A morning pickup is best, because that will give the puppy all day to explore his new surroundings.

Keep Puppy Safe

Although it may be tempting to show off your cute little guy, do not expose your puppy to friends or neighbors (and especially their dogs) until he's had his vaccinations. Dogs can transmit diseases to other dogs, and people can carry bacteria on their hands or clothes that can be passed to the puppy. Until he's had his vaccinations, it is best to limit visitors, both canine and human.

Owning a puppy can teach your child responsibility and respect for animals.

If the puppy is only a short car ride away, you should bring a small cardboard box or a crate to place him in, a blanket to keep him warm, and towels to clean up any messes. Puppies tend to get carsick, especially if it is their first ride, so he may throw up or urinate. Keeping the car well ventilated may help avoid these situations. Also, be sure to tell the breeder what time you will be picking the puppy up, so she can plan his meals accordingly.

If it is a longer car ride, plan to make frequent stops. Bring along his collar and leash so you can take him out to exercise and to relieve himself. Do not let him around other dogs or in areas where other dogs have been are until he gets all of his vaccinations, however.

Before you leave the breeder, there are certain documents that she should provide you with that will include important and necessary information, including a vaccination record, a pedigree, a registration certificate, a diet sheet, and a health guarantee.

What is a Pedigree?

All purebred dogs have a pedigree. The pedigree does not imply that a dog is of show quality, but is simply a chronological list of ancestors. Also, registration papers only guarantee that a dog is a particular breed, nothing else. Neither paper is a guarantee of the health or the quality of your dog.

The First Few Days

The first few days that a puppy spends away from his mother and littermates may be frightening for him. He is in a strange environment, with new sounds and new people, and he will probably feel scared, insecure, and lonely. It is very important to try to make him as comfortable as possible, which is why it's a good

Have all the supplies you will need, such as a bed, food and water bowls, and a collar and leash, ready for your puppy when he arrives.

Your new puppy will need extra love and attention his first nights in his new home.

idea to take some time off to spend with him. During the day, try to refrain from overwhelming him with new people or things and allow him to adjust and explore your home at his own pace. Introduce him right away to the schedule that you have set up for him so that he becomes used to the routine.

Your puppy may whimper or cry at night. For the first couple of nights, you should comfort him by providing him with a warm blanket, soft toys, and a dim nightlight. However, don't let him do anything now that you are not planning to let him do in the future. For example, if you do not want him to sleep on the bed or the furniture, don't allow him to do so now. However, you might bring his bed or crate into your room so he can be near you. As the days pass, he will become used to his new environment and should become more comfortable.

Quick Tip to Ease Adjustment

Here's a tip to help your puppy adjust to his new home: Allow your puppy to sleep with a few articles of your clothing, preferably something you have worn and that smells like you. This way, your puppy will become adjusted to your scent and will feel more comfortable in his new environment.

The worst thing you can do to a scared puppy is to yell at him or scold him for making noise or crying. This will only make matters worse and teach your puppy to fear you instead of trust you. Remember that each puppy is an individual and will need different levels of attention. It is important to find a balance between coddling and comforting.

Now your puppy is home safe and sound; he may even be getting to like it. But your journey is just beginning. Remember that you are responsible for all the aspects of this little guy's care—mentally and physically—and you must teach him how to behave in your home and in the world.

Caring for Your Puppy

As a puppy owner, you'll discover that the one thing that your puppy loves the most (besides you, of course) is food. Good nutrition is a necessary requirement in a puppy's life. Providing your puppy with the proper diet is one of the most important aspects of caring for him. By carefully researching which diet is the best, you can ensure that his good health will affect all other parts of your life together.

Dog Foods

If you take a trip to your local pet emporium or supermarket, you cannot help but notice that there is an overwhelming selection of dog foods available. It can be confusing, to say the least, and it makes it hard to choose which brand is best for your puppy. There are certain things you should know about commercial dog food that will help you to make the right decision. The more you educate yourself about what your puppy's nutritional needs are and how dog food is manufactured, the easier the decision will be.

Water, Water!

Water is the most important of all nutrients, and all dogs must retain a water balance, which means that their total intake of water should be in balance with the total output.

Make sure that your puppy has access to cool, clean water at all times.

First, you should pick a dog food that is specially formulated for puppies. This will ensure that your pup is getting the proper nutrition for growth and digestion for his undeveloped systems.

As a new owner, you will be responsible for all your puppy's needs.

There are three types of dog food available on the market today, and all of them have good points and bad points. You must choose the type that best fits your puppy's needs.

First Meals

If you are lucky, the breeder or shelter from which you obtained your puppy will have given you a diet sheet, which will help you immensely with your feeding chores. A diet sheet will typically tell you the type of food your puppy has been eating, when he eats, and how to increase his

Dog Food Differences at a Glance

Dry Food

Upside—Least expensive, can conveniently be left in bowl for longer periods of time, helps control tartar

Downside—Least appealing to dogs

Canned Food

Upside—Most appealing to dogs

Downside—Spoils quickly, expensive, requires more to be fed because energy content is relatively low, especially for large breeds

Semi-Moist

Upside—Will not spoil at room temperature, comes in prepackaged servings

Downside—Contains large amounts of sugar and preservatives in order to maintain freshness without refrigeration

food intake as he ages. Some breeders will even include enough food to get you through a day or two. You should follow this original feeding schedule as closely as possible and use the same brand of puppy food for the first few months.

If no diet sheet was provided for you, you will have to use the information available about dog food and choose one that is specially formulated for puppies. It should indicate that it is a growth formula. If you are undecided about which brand to choose, your veterinarian can make a recommendation.

When to Feed

Your puppy will need to start off with light, frequent meals because his stomach is so small. If the breeder has included a feeding schedule with your diet sheet, you should follow that as closely as possible and make increases or decreases whenever she recommends.

In the beginning, feed your puppy the same brand of dog food as the breeder in order to avoid stomach problems.

If no feeding schedule accompanied your puppy, you should put him on one right away.

You should feed a puppy that is four months of age or younger four times a day. From four to six months of age, you can reduce the feedings to three times a day, and after six months, you can start feeding once or twice a day, depending on your schedule. You should always feed him at the same time of day—preferably starting out with breakfast, lunch, mid-afternoon snack, and dinner, which

Doggy Vegetarians?

Unlike cats, dogs are not true carnivores and can exist on a vegetarian diet. They can convert vegetable fat and protein into the ingredients that they need to perform bodily functions. However, you should consult a veterinarian before switching your dog to a vegetarian diet, because it is a lot of work to maintain balanced nutrition.

Say No to Chocolate

It may seem harmless to feed your puppy sweets, but chocolate can cause your dog to become seriously ill or even die. The two chemicals in chocolate, caffeine and theobromine, overstimulate the puppy's nervous system, especially in small-sized dogs—10 ounces of chocolate can kill a 12-pound dog! Symptoms of chocolate poisoning include restlessness, vomiting, increased heart rate, seizure, and coma. If your dog has ingested chocolate, you can give syrup of ipecac at a dosage of one-eighth of a teaspoon per pound to induce vomiting and get your puppy to the veterinarian immediately.

should be served an hour before bedtime. He should be taken outside to do his business as soon as he is finished his meal.

How Much to Feed

If you don't know the puppy's prior feeding schedule, you will have to figure out how much to feed him. Start off by following the

Your puppy should be fed a good-quality dog food that is nutritious and for-mulated for his stage of life.

Caring for Your Puppy

directions on the dog food label and increasing or decreasing the amount as needed. Put down the recommended amount for your puppy's age and take it away after a period of time. If your puppy eats his food quickly and leaves nothing in his bowl, you need to increase the amount. If he leaves food in his bowl, you may have to decrease the amount or feed smaller meals more frequently.

Quick & Easy Checklist for Feeding

- Do provide your puppy with dog food made for his stage in life from a reputable manufacturer.
- Do have fresh water available for your puppy at all times.
- Do serve your puppy's food at room temperature.
- Do watch your puppy's weight.
- Do call your veterinarian if your puppy refuses to eat in a 24-hour period.
- Do feed your puppy nutritious snacks.
- Don't allow children to bother the puppy when he is eating.
- Don't offer spoiled or stale food to your dog.
- Don't change your puppy's diet suddenly.
- Don't leave any uneaten canned or moist food out after your dog is finished eating his meal and discard dry food at the end of each day.
- Don't allow your dog to have brittle bones, like chicken bones, or unhealthy snacks.
- Don't feed your puppy first. Having him eat after you will help to establish your dominant role.

Treats

Treats are a great way to encourage and reward your puppy when he has done something well. There are plenty of treats available today that are not only tasty but nutritious, and hard biscuits can help

If you give your puppy treats, make sure they are healthy and do not upset his regular diet.

keep his teeth clean. However, use common sense and moderation. Remember to consider his treats as part of his total food intake. Limit the amount of treats you give your puppy and be sure to feed him only healthy snacks. Avoid giving him table scraps, because they are usually not good for him and just add to his caloric intake. Obesity is a very serious health problem in dogs, so be sure to start your puppy off eating right.

Bones

Bones can help your puppy with his overwhelming need to chew, keep his teeth clean, and him keep from becoming bored. Just make sure you give your dog the right kind of bones to keep him safe. You should give your puppy toys and bones made especially for dogs that will not splinter or break into tiny pieces. These pieces can be swallowed and become stuck in your puppy's intestinal tract or cause him to choke. There are plenty of manufacturers that make

If you start grooming your dog while he is a puppy, he will soon become accustomed to the procedure.

safe chewable and edible dog bones, so do your puppy a favor and give him something both fun and safe as a special treat.

Grooming Your Puppy

Your puppy will rely on you to care for him and keep him healthy. This means he will rely on you to ensure that he is kept clean, brushed, and looking his best, which can be done easily with regular grooming. Grooming is also important because it gives you a chance to inspect your dog and catch any skin or health problems before they start. Every dog, no matter what his breed, will require grooming, and some breeds will require more attention than others.

In order to keep your dog looking good, you need to have the right tools. There is a large selection of grooming equipment available for every coat type, but there are some universal tools that every owner should have in order to perform general grooming duties, such as a brush, comb, nail clippers, and dog shampoo.

Puppyhood is the best time to start grooming procedures, because your dog will more easily become used to the grooming routine and soon come to expect it as part of his everyday life. This is especially true if you have a dog that requires extensive grooming or if you plan to show your puppy when he gets older. It is best to start out

Most puppies require only an occasional bath, but dogs with longer coats may need to be bathed more often.

Caring for Your Puppy

slowly so that he doesn't become overwhelmed or frightened, and then build on grooming time until you have the whole routine down pat.

Brushing

Brushing on a daily basis will go a long way to keeping your dog looking good. Daily brushing will reduce shedding, keep mats to a minimum, and allow you to inspect his coat for any foreign debris or skin problems. It also stimulates your dog's skin and spreads the coat's natural oils, which help keep his coat shiny and his skin healthy. Puppies that are brushed on a routine basis will need to be bathed less often, because most of the dirt and debris in his coat will be removed regularly.

Each coat type will require a different amount of brushing. Dogs with short or smooth coats, such as hounds, can be gone over with a grooming glove a few times a week; however, a dog with a long, silky coat like a Yorkshire Terrier will need daily brushing to keep mats away.

Trim your puppy's nails and inspect his feet for any injuries on a regular basis.

Bathing

Most puppies will require a bath only occasionally, every few months or so. Healthy dogs are pretty good at keeping themselves clean, and regular brushing should keep your puppy's coat in good shape. Some dogs have waterproof coats, and it is best not to bathe them too often because it can strip the natural oils and reduce the coat's ability to repel

Tub Tricks

If your dog has had a previously bad experience in the tub, it may be almost impossible to get him in there at bath time. The trick is to make it as fun and rewarding as possible for your puppy. One owner always leaves treats for her English Springer Spaniel on the sides of the tub and lets him eat them while he's being bathed. Now all she has to say is "Bath time" and he runs and jumps right in.

water. In fact, overbathing your dog can cause dry skin and irritation, which can cause excess scratching or infections. But at some time, every puppy will roll in something particularly smelly or dirty and require a bath.

Nail and Foot Care

It is important to take good care of your puppy's paws. Always examine your puppy's feet as part of his daily grooming routine. Inspect your dog's feet after each outing and check that there are no sharp objects, burrs, thorns, seeds, or splinters in the pads or between the toes. If you find anything, remove it gently with a pair of tweezers. Also watch for soreness or blisters. If your puppy shows any signs of soreness or favors a leg when he walks, take him to the veterinarian immediately.

Nail trimming is something that your dog should get used to in puppyhood. The earlier your puppy gets used to having his nails trimmed, the easier your life will be at grooming time. Trimming your puppy's nails is not as hard as it may seem. The easiest way to do it is with a pair of canine nail clippers. You can also use an electric nail grinder, if you find this method easier. You need to cut the nail to just the point where it begins, taking care to avoid the quick, which is the area of the nail that contains nerves and blood vessels. If you accidentally cut the quick of his nail, it will bleed and will be painful to your dog.

If it makes you too nervous to trim your puppy's nails, don't ignore the task. Hand him over to an experienced groomer and let her do it for you. But if you start now and add it to your weekly schedule, you and your puppy will be nail-trimming experts in no time.

Ear Care

Do not neglect your puppy's ears when going through your grooming steps, because it is very important to his health. Ear infections can be caused by excessive dirt, moisture, and bacteria accumulating in the ear canal.

The first thing you should do is pluck or trim (with blunt-nosed scissors) the excess hair out. To keep the ears clean, use a cotton ball or washcloth dampened with commercial ear cleaner or mineral oil and wipe the inside of the earflap. If your puppy's ear is sore, has excess wax, or has a bad smell, he probably has an ear infection and needs to see the veterinarian immediately.

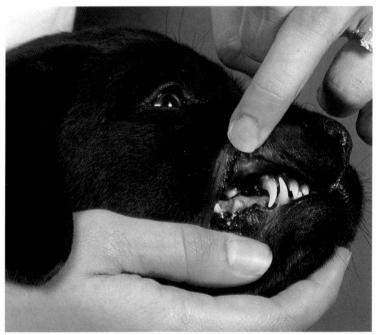

Examine your puppy's teeth on a regular basis.

Quick & Easy Puppy Care and Training

Dental Care

Puppies need to chew. Chewing is an essential part of their physical and mental development, so you need to take good care of their teeth from the very beginning.

If you do not brush your dog's teeth on a regular basis, plaque builds up on the teeth and under the gums. If this plaque is not removed, periodontal disease, which is a bacterial infection, can occur. If left untreated, the bacteria can enter the bloodstream and spread to your puppy's vital organs. Other problems can develop as well, such as mouth abscesses and tooth loss. Also, puppies that don't receive good dental care can suffer from really bad breath, a feature that does not endear them to humans or elicit doggy kisses.

It is much easier to brush your puppy's teeth than you may think, as long as you have the right supplies. You should purchase a dog toothbrush or a finger toothbrush (a rubber cap that fits over your index finger) and toothpaste made for dogs. Start by accustoming your puppy to having your fingers in his mouth without brushing his teeth. When you are giving him his daily once-over, be sure to look in his mouth, lift his dewflaps to expose his gums, and touch his teeth. Soon this will become just another part of his grooming routine.

Not for Dogs!

Never use human toothpaste when brushing your puppy's teeth. Dogs will not spit out the toothpaste, like humans do, but will swallow it, which can cause stomach upset and digestive problems. Also, the minty taste that humans enjoy probably will not be as appealing to your puppy as it is to you. Canine toothpaste comes in "doggy-friendly" flavors, such as beef and poultry, and are edible.

Once he is used to this procedure, put some doggy-flavored toothpaste on the toothbrush and gently rub a few teeth at a time. Be sure to brush the tooth at the gum line.

Use a circular motion when brushing and slowly make your way around your dog's upper teeth. Make sure to get the teeth in the back of the mouth, because these are the ones most prone to periodontal disease. When you are finished with the top, do the bottom in the same manner.

Daily brushing would be ideal, but try to do it at least four times a week. This will ensure that your puppy keeps his teeth healthy and keeps them for a long time. You can also promote dental health by giving your puppy chew toys that help fight plaque and strengthen jaws. Good examples are Nylabone® Rhinos® and Dental Chews®.

Housetraining Your Puppy

One of the first forms of training that you and your puppy will undertake will be housetraining. Housetraining means that you are teaching your dog that he has a specific place that he should eliminate, usually outside. Your best bet is to start housetraining him as soon as you get him home. However, you need to remember that puppies between the ages of 8 to 16 weeks will not have control of their bladders or bowels. They will not be able to "hold it" until they get a little older. This means that in the beginning, housetraining will take vigilance on your part. You will have to watch your puppy very carefully for signs that he needs to eliminate. He will most likely have to go to the bathroom after eating, drinking,

Potty On Command

If you start the housetraining process early enough, you can teach your puppy to go to the bathroom on command. When you take your puppy outside, use a command while he is eliminating. A couple of suggestions include "potty time," "hurry up," or "do your business." Use any command that you are comfortable saying. Use this command every time you take your puppy to the bathroom. Soon, he will get used to hearing the command, and will go when you tell him to. This way, you won't be left standing in the cold.

sleeping, and playing. Most puppies will also give off signals, like circling or sniffing the floor—these behaviors are a sure sign that your puppy needs to get outside. When you see him display this behavior, don't hesitate. Pick him up and carry him outside to the place where you want him to eliminate. As he is doing his business, tell him what a good boy he is.

Make sure your puppy has ample time outside to eliminate. This will cut down on the number of accidents he has in the house.

Pretty soon, with the help of a regular schedule, you will be able to predict the times that your puppy will need to eliminate. The most useful thing that you can buy for your puppy to help facilitate this process is a crate. Training your puppy to use the crate is the quickest and easiest way to housetrain your dog. Just remember that your puppy will be picking up habits throughout his training that will last him his lifetime— make sure that he picks up the right ones.

Quick & Easy Puppy Care and Training

If your puppy becomes accustomed to his Fold-Away Pet Carrier™ at an early age, he will soon think of it as his home away from home.

Crate Training

By about five weeks of age, most puppies are starting to move away from their mom and littermates to relieve themselves. This instinct to keep the bed clean is the basis of crate training. Crates work well because your puppy will not want to soil where he eats and sleeps.

Quick and Easy Space Saver

A crate is a very important training tool, and when used properly, can become a second home to your dog. However, that second home can take up a lot of space in your home, which is why the Fold-Away Pet Carrier™ is so useful. It's a kind of crate/carrier combo that's strong enough for airline travel and, when not in use, it easy folds for storage in a closet or under a bed. When you need it, it can be put together in no time.

Crate Don'ts

- Don"t let your puppy out of the crate if he starts crying or scratching at the door. If you let him out after he complains, he will think that complaining will get him released every time. The best thing to do if your puppy is having a temper tantrum in his crate is to ignore him. Only let him out when he is quiet and has calmed down.

- Don't use the crate as punishment. If you put your puppy in his crate when he does something bad, he will recognize your criticism and sense your anger, and he will come to think of his crate as a bad place. Even if you are angry at your dog and want to get him out of the way, make sure that you praise him for going into his crate and give him a treat or toy.

They also like to curl up in small dark places that offer them protection on three sides, because it makes them feel more secure. When you provide your puppy with a crate, you are giving him his very own "den."

Establish a daily eating, drinking, and outside schedule for your puppy. This will help you to predict when he will need to eliminate.

He will do his best to eliminate away from his den, and in effect, away from your house.

Being confined in the crate will help your puppy develop better bowel and bladder control. When he is confined for gradually extended periods of time, he will learn to hold his wastes to avoid soiling his bed. It is your responsibility to make sure that he is given plenty of time outside the crate and outside the house, or the training process will not be successful.

Quick & Easy Puppy Care and Training

Puppy Umbilical Cord

One way to constantly supervise your puppy is to use what some trainers call the puppy umbilical cord. Start by attaching one end of a long leash to your puppy's collar and the other end to you. Now everywhere that you go, he goes, and vice versa. This method will help prevent accidents because you'll notice any signs that your puppy has to go outside much quicker.

Outside Schedule

As was mentioned before, puppies need time to develop bowel and bladder control. The best way to most accurately predict when your puppy needs to eliminate is to establish a routine that works well for both of you and stick to it. If you make a daily schedule of eating, drinking, and outside time and stick to it, you will see your puppy progress.

Every person and family will have a different routine—there is no one right schedule for everyone. Just make sure that you arrange times and duties that everyone can stick with. The schedule you set up will have to work with your normal routine and lifestyle.

The following is an example of a schedule that might work for you and your family, but remember that any schedule can work as long as you can give your dog the necessary attention.

7:00 am—Take the puppy outside (this time might be even earlier for young puppies who have a hard time holding it all night). After the puppy relieves himself, praise him and bring him inside. Fix the puppy's breakfast, offer him water, and then send him out in the backyard while you get ready to start the day.

8:00 am—Go outside to play with the puppy for a few minutes before leaving for the day. Just before you leave, bring the puppy inside, put him in his crate, and give him a treat and a toy to keep him occupied.

Housetraining Your Puppy   33

Be sure to provide your puppy with cool, clean water, especially when outside.

12:00 am—If at all possible, this would be a good time to come home for lunch, let your puppy out of his crate, and take him outside to eliminate. If you or another family member can't do it, try to find a neighbor (a retired person or stay-at-home mom might be a good idea) to come over. Take this time to play with your puppy and give him a little exercise.

3:00 pm—If you have school-aged children, make sure one of them comes straight home from school to take the puppy outside, walk him, and play with him for a while. After playing, let the puppy hang out with your child while he or she does homework or watches television. If you do not have kids, you may be able to pay a teenager in your neighborhood to come over after school.

6:00 pm—If you are just arriving home and your puppy has been confined for a few hours, immediately let him outside to eliminate and play. After you eat your own dinner, feed him his dinner and take the puppy outside to go potty.

8:00 pm—After some quality family time (puppy included), groom your puppy, offer him some water, and then takes him outside to go potty.

11:00 pm—Take the puppy outside to go potty one last time before going to bed.

Preventing Accidents

Puppies often sniff out the same spot to eliminate. This is a good thing if you have taught him to go to a special place in your yard; a bad thing if he previously has gone in your living room. If your puppy does eliminate in your house, make sure you clean it up right away with a pet-odor neutralizer, which can be bought in a pet store. You can also scrub the area thoroughly with a solution of one-fourth cup of white vinegar and a squirt of liquid detergent mixed with a quart of warm water.

Keep in mind that your puppy should not remain in the crate for longer than three to four hours at a time, except during the night. In addition, the puppy will need to relieve himself after waking up, after eating, after playtime, and every three to four hours in between.

Accidents Will Happen

There is a very important thing that you should remember when house-training your dog: If the puppy relieves himself in the house, it is not his fault, it's yours. If your puppy has an accident, it means that the puppy was not supervised well enough or that he wasn't taken outside in time.

Prevent accidents from happening by keeping your puppy in an enclosed area and supervising him at all times.

If you catch him in the act of relieving himself, don't yell or scold him. Simply say "No!" loudly, which should startle him enough to stop him, pick him up, take him outside, and let him continue in his regular relief area. Then praise him for finishing outside. If you scold or punish him, you are not teaching him where he needs to relieve himself. Instead, you are teaching him that you think going potty is wrong. Because he has to go, he will then become sneaky about it, and you will find puddles and piles in strange places. Don't concentrate on correcting him; emphasize the praise for going potty in the right place.

If you happen to find a little surprise left for you, do not yell at your puppy for it and never rub his nose in it. Your puppy will have no idea what you are talking about, and you'll only make him scared of you. Simply clean it up and be sure to keep a closer eye on him next time.

Housetraining is one of the most important gifts that you can give your dog. It allows them to live as one of the family. Every puppy will make mistakes, especially in the beginning. Do not worry—with the proper training and lots of patience, every dog can be housetrained.

Basic Training for Good Behavior

Training is important, because good basic training will transform your jumpy, squirmy, wiggly little puppy into a well-mannered dog that is a joy to be around. A puppy has the right to be trained—it is unfair to leave him to figure out the human world all on his own, and he won't be able to do it.

You, too, will benefit from training, because you will learn how to motivate your puppy. You will also learn how to prevent problem behavior and how to correct mistakes that do happen. Puppy training entails much more than learning the traditional sit, down, stay, and come commands—it means that you will

Let your puppy get used to his collar by allowing him to wear it for short periods of time.

be teaching your puppy that he's living in your house, not his. You can set some rules and expect him to follow them.

Collar and Leash Training

Training a puppy to his collar and leash is very easy and is something you can start doing right away. Place a soft nylon collar on the puppy. He will initially try to bite at it, but he will soon forget it's there—the more so if you play with him. Some people leave their dog's collar on all of the time, others put it on only when they are taking the dog out. If it is to be left on, purchase a narrow or round one so it does not mark the fur or become snagged on furniture.

Once the puppy ignores his collar, you can attach the leash to it and let him pull the leash behind him for a few minutes every day. However, if the pup starts to chew at the leash, simply keep it slack and let him go where he wants. The idea is to let him get the feel of the leash, but not get in the habit of chewing it. Repeat this a couple of times a day for two days, and the pup will get used to the leash without thinking that it will restrain him.

Puppy Kindergarten

The next step in your puppy's training is to attend a class geared just for him. Puppy kindergarten classes consist of obedience training and socialization and are for puppies between the ages of 10 and 16 weeks. A puppy owner also learns how to prevent problem behaviors from occurring and how to establish household rules. Every puppy can benefit from taking this type of class. It will teach the basic foundations of training, as well as provide an excellent opportunity for your puppy to socialize with other dogs and people. A good puppy kindergarten class will teach you how to train your dog and help to teach your dog the basic obedience commands, like come, sit, stay, down, and heel. Participating in a kindergarten class with your puppy will strengthen the bond between you, bring you closer together, and help you to learn the right way to train your dog. After your puppy passes puppy kindergarten—the sky's the limit!

Puppy kindergarten is a great place to teach your pup basic obedience, as well as socialize him with other dogs.

Basic Commands

Although your puppy should attend puppy kindergarten if at all possible, you can begin training your puppy yourself as soon as he is comfortable in your home and knows his name. It is also very helpful to take the lessons that you learn together in kindergarten and practice them at home. Doing your "homework" together will not only reinforce what you learn in class, it will allow you to spend some quality one-on-one time with your pup.

There are two very important things to remember when training your puppy: first, train the puppy away from any potential distractions, and second, keep all lessons very short. Eliminating any distraction is important because it is essential that you have the full attention of your puppy. This is not possible if there are other people around, radios on, or other dogs, butterflies, or birds to play with.

Before beginning a lesson, always play a little game with the puppy so that he is in an active state of mind and more receptive to the matter at hand. Likewise, always end a lesson with fun time for the

Your puppy should always associate coming to you with pleasant things, such as toys, praise, and treats.

pup, and always end training on a high note, praising the puppy. End the lesson when the pup has done as you require so that he receives lots of praise. This will really build his confidence.

The Come Command

The come command is possibly the most important command you can teach your puppy—it may even save his life someday. Knowing that your dog will come to you immediately when you call him will ensure that you can trust him to return to you if there is any kind of danger nearby. The most important thing to remember when teaching your puppy to come when called is that it should always be a pleasant experience. You should never call your puppy to you to scold or yell at him. If you call him to punish him, he will soon learn not to respond to the command.

Quick & Easy Tricks to Teach "Come"

Puppyhood is the easiest time to teach your dog the come command, because most puppies want to be near you anyway. Take advantage of this natural reaction and start teaching the come command as soon as you get your puppy home. Whenever your puppy decides to run to you, just give him the come command. Even if he was going to do it anyway, he will learn to associate the action with the words, and it will reinforce your position as the pack leader.

Start with your puppy on a long lead (about 20 feet in length). Have plenty of small, tasty treats with you. Walk the distance of the lead, then crouch down and call your puppy to you. Make sure that you use a happy, excited tone of voice when you use his name. Your puppy should come to you enthusiastically. If he does not, use the long lead to pull him toward you, but continue to use the happy tone of voice. Your puppy should learn from the start that coming when you call him is not an option.

Basic Training for Good Behavior 41

Your puppy must wear a collar and be on his leash when outdoors, for his safety and for the safety of others.

No matter how he gets to you, give him lots of praise and a treat when he gets there. Continue to use the long lead until your puppy is consistently obeying your command.

The Sit Command

There are two ways to teach the sit command. First, get a treat that your dog really likes and hold it right by his nose, so that all his attention is focused on it. Raise the treat above his head and tell him to sit. Usually, the puppy will follow the treat above his head and automatically sit down. Give him the treat for being such a good boy and don't forget to praise him. After a while, he will begin to associate the word "sit" with his action. Most puppies will get the gist very quickly. Once he is sitting reliably with the treat, take it away and just use praise as a reward when he obeys.

However, there are some puppies that are more obstinate than others, and they may need a little more encouragement to get the picture. If your puppy doesn't sit automatically when the treat is over his nose, place one hand on his hindquarters and the other under his upper chest. Say, "Sit" in a pleasant (never harsh) voice, and at the same time, lightly push down on his rear end and push up under his chest until he is sitting. Now lavish praise on the puppy and give him the treat. Repeat this a few times, and your pet will get the idea.

The Stay Command

This command should follow your sit lesson, but it can be very hard for puppies to get the hang of. Remember that your puppy wants nothing more than to be at your side, so it will be hard for him to stay in one place while you walk away. You should only expect him to perform this

The sit command is the foundation for all other training, and your puppy should have no trouble mastering it.

command for a few seconds at first, and then gradually work up to longer periods of time.

Face the puppy and tell him to sit. Now step backward, and as you do, say, "Stay." It is also very helpful to use the hand signal for stay—place your hand straight out, palm toward the dog's nose. Let the pup remain in the position for only a few seconds before calling him to you and giving lots of praise and a treat. Once he gets the hang of it, repeat the command again, but step farther back. If the

Long(er) Stays

As the weeks go by, you can increase the length of time the pup is left in the stay position—but two to three minutes is quite long enough for a puppy. If your puppy drops into a lying position and is clearly more comfortable, there is nothing wrong with it. In the beginning, staying put is good enough!

pup gets up and comes to you, simply place him back in the original position and start again. As he starts to understand the command, you can move farther and farther back.

The Down Command

There are two ways to teach this command. Obviously, with a puppy, it will be easier to get your dog to go down if you are kneeling next to him. If your dog is more willing to please, the first method should work: Have your dog sit and hold a treat in front of his nose. When his full attention is on the treat, start to lower the treat slowly to the ground, while saying, "Down." He should follow the treat with his head. Then bring it out slowly in front of him. If you are really lucky, your puppy will slide his legs forward and lie down by himself. Then he gets the treat and lots of praise for being such a good boy. If he won't lie down on his own (and most puppies won't), you can try this method: After the puppy is sitting and focused on the treat, take each of his front legs and gently sweep them forward, at the same time saying, "Down." Release the legs

Once your puppy masters the basic commands, like the down command, he can go on to more advanced obedience training.

Keep Things Simple

Don't confuse your puppy by using the down command for anything other than lying down. For example, if you want him to get off the couch, use another word, like "off," to get your point across. This way when you go to teach him the down command, there will be no doubt in his mind what you expect from him.

and quickly apply light pressure on the shoulders with your left hand. Then quickly tell him he is a good boy, give him the treat, and make a lot of fuss. Repeat two or three times only in one training session. The pup will learn over a few lessons. Remember that this is a very submissive act on the pup's behalf, so there is no need to rush matters.

The Heel Command

All dogs should be able to walk nicely on a leash without their owners being involved in a tug-of-war. Teaching your puppy the heel command should follow leash training. Heeling is best done in a place where you have a wall or a fence to one side of you, because it will restrict the puppy's lateral movements so that you only have to contend with forward and backward situations. Again, it is better to do the lesson in private and not in a place where there will be many distractions.

Hold the leash in your right hand and pass it through your left. As the puppy moves ahead and strains on the leash, give a quick jerk backward with your left hand, while at the same time saying, "Heel." You want the pup's chest to be level with or just behind an imaginary line from your knee. When the puppy is in this position, praise him and begin walking again. Keep repeating the whole exercise. Once the puppy begins to get the message, then you can use your left hand (with the treat inside of it) to pat the side of your knee so that the pup is encouraged to keep close to your side.

If you teach your puppy good leash manners, he can accompany you on all sorts of fun adventures.

Solving Problems

Dogs will be dogs. Behaviors that we may consider to be "problems" are often just puppies doing what puppies do. Things like barking, digging, and jumping up are natural instincts to your puppy. You must teach your puppy how you want him to behave in your home—he will not know automatically.

There are some common puppy behaviors that may cause problems in your house. The good news is that with the proper training and motivation, they can be dealt with easily.

Barking

Some owners think that they want their dog to bark—that it makes the puppy a good watchdog. However, this is a habit that should not be encouraged. Most dogs will bark anyway when a stranger comes to the door or into their territory. What you don't want is a dog that barks at every car that drives by or every leaf that falls into the yard. This is not only annoying to you, but to the surrounding neighborhood.

Health-Related Problems

If your dog has some behavior problems, they may not be due to a lack of training. Some experts feel that 20 percent of all behavior problems are caused by health-related problems. Housetraining accidents could be caused by bladder infections or gastrointestinal upset, and medical problems like thyroid imbalance can cause hyperactivity. Poor nutrition can also be a factor. Chewing on garden plants or wood could indicate that your puppy is not getting enough nutrients, and food allergies are often the cause of behavior problems. Before you start training your dog, make sure that he has been to the veterinarian and has received a clean bill of health. Once health problems have been ruled out, you can start correcting any unwanted behavior.

Overzealous barking is an inherited tendency, but a lot of puppy barking is due to boredom. If your puppy barks when he wants attention or when he is left alone, you can take steps to stop it. If you notice your puppy barks for attention, you must not reinforce the bad behavior. Never give him attention when he is barking. Wait until he is quiet and then pet and praise him. If he starts barking again, walk away and ignore him. Your puppy should get the picture in no time.

If you notice that he barks when he is left alone (or if your angry neighbors inform you that he barks when he's left alone), there are a few things you can try. Before you leave, see that all his needs are met, and that he has been walked, fed, and watered. Be sure to allow him to get plenty of exercise before you leave—a sleeping puppy will not be a barking puppy. Make sure your curb his boredom by providing him with lots of toys to play with while you're gone. These should satisfy his need to chew, which is a way for dogs to relieve boredom. A Nylabone® Rhino smeared with peanut butter or soft cheese will hold his attention for hours. Leave a radio on an easy-listening station to keep him company. If he barks at things

Toys—like this Rhino™ chew— will help to keep your puppy's teeth clean while keeping him out of mischief.

outside, pull the shades or close the curtains. Eventually, he will get used to his time alone, especially if he's having fun all by himself.

Jumping Up

A puppy that jumps up is a happy puppy. However, while it's cute while he is small, few guests appreciate dogs jumping on them, especially when your sweet little Great Dane pup continues this habit into adulthood. There will come a time, probably around four months of age, that your puppy will need to know when it is okay to jump and when he should show off his good manners by sitting instead. How do you correct the problem? All family members need to participate in teaching the puppy to sit as soon as he starts to jump up. You'll need to have someone keep puppy on his leash while someone else greets him so that he can be distracted and helped to sit. The person greeting the puppy should not pay him any attention until he is sitting. When he sits and is greeted, that is his reward. Remember that the entire family must take part. Each time you allow him to jump up, you go back a step in training, because your puppy will not understand that it is okay to jump on Dad but not okay to jump on Grandma.

Biting and Nipping

All puppies bite and try to chew on your fingers, toes, arms, etc. This is the time to teach them to be gentle and not bite hard. Put your fingers in your puppy's mouth, and if he bites too hard, cry out like his littermate would. Let him know he's hurting you by squealing and acting like you have been seriously hurt. Don't pull your hand away too quickly as this can instigate a desire to bring down "prey." He should release your hand when he hears you cry. If he does, say "Good drop." Do not continue to play

Your puppy wants nothing more than to please you. Praise and affection are the best training motivators for your dog.

with the puppy until he has calmed down. If the puppy continues to play too rough and doesn't respond to your corrections, then he needs "time out" in his crate.

Do not allow your puppy to develop habits that you may later find unacceptable, such as biting or nipping. Establish household rules from the beginning and stick to them.

Basic Training for Good Behavior 49

Biting Hard

Your dog must know who is in charge. If aggressive biting occurs, you should seek professional help at once. Professional help through your veterinarian, dog trainer, and/or behaviorist can give you guidance.

Digging

Bored dogs release their frustrations through mischievous behavior such as digging. Puppies shouldn't be left unattended outside for long periods of time, even if they are in a fenced-in yard. Usually the puppy is sent to the backyard because the owner cannot tolerate him in the house. The culprit feels socially deprived and feels the need to be included in his owner's life. The puppy only wants to develop into the companion that you desired when you got him in the first place. Let your puppy in the house and allow him to participate in family activities as much as possible.

The Runaway

If your puppy is never let off his leash except when supervised in a fenced-in yard, he should not be able to do much running away. However, there is always the dog that seems to have been an escape artist in another life and he will get out no matter how diligent you are.

Problem Solver: A Dog Run

If you do need to leave your dog outside unattended and do not want your yard to look like a mine field, the best solution is to build your puppy a dog run. Fence off a space that will be large enough for him to have room to move about when he is fully grown. Provide shelter, food, and water and keep it stocked with lots of bones and toys. This way, your puppy will get to enjoy time outside without you having to worry about what he will get into.

Provide your puppy with a safe, fenced-in yard to play in while outside.

Perhaps your puppy escapes or perhaps you are playing with him in the yard and he refuses to come when called. You now have a runaway. If your puppy is not in immediate danger, the best thing to do is to use a little reverse psychology. Do not chase him. He will just think that you are playing a game with him and will run away further. Use what you know about your little guy—namely that he loves to be with you. He will never want to think that he is missing out on the fun. Try calling his name in a happy, excited tone of voice and then running in the opposite direction. Most likely, your curious puppy will want in on the game and start to follow you. You can then turn around and call him to you. Always kneel down when trying to catch the runaway, because dogs can be intimidated by people standing over them. It is always helpful to have a treat or a favorite toy to help entice him to your side.

Remember that when you finally do catch your naughty dog, you must not discipline him. After all, it is quite possible there could be a repeat performance, and it would be nice if the next time he would respond to your come command.

Basic Training for Good Behavior 51

Training will give your dog the direction he needs to live a happy life with his family.

The Right to Be Trained

Every puppy not only needs basic training—he deserves it. A dog will not know automatically how he should behave. He deserves to have knowledge of the rules that he is supposed to follow. He is entitled to know what is expected of him. He has the right to learn the basic tools in order to fit in with his new family. Once your puppy knows all these things, he will be perfectly willing to do what he has to do in order to fit in with his family pack.

Training will give him the direction he needs to live a happy life with his human family. When you provide him with this opportunity, you are ensuring that you and your puppy will get along beautifully for the duration of your life together.

Puppy Health Care

You can ensure your puppy's good health by being a responsible owner and providing him with everything he needs to maintain his well-being. The better care you take of your puppy now, while he is young, the longer you'll have him around to enjoy. You want your pup's years with you to be happy ones.

The First Checkup

You will want to take your new puppy in for his first checkup within 48 to 72 hours after acquiring him. A puppy can appear healthy at first, but he may have a serious problem that is not immediately apparent. Most pets have some type of a minor flaw

Regular veterinary visits are necessary to maintain your puppy's good health throughout his lifetime.

Quick & Easy Puppy Care and Training

Puppies receive maternal antibodies in the first few weeks of life that protect them from disease; vaccinations are necessary because the antibodies are only temporarily effective.

that may never cause a real problem. Unfortunately, if he has a serious problem, you may want to consider the consequences of keeping the pet. Especially if you have children, attachments will be formed that may have to be broken prematurely.

At the first visit, your veterinarian will check your pet's overall condition, which includes listening to the heart; checking the respiration; feeling the abdomen, muscles, and joints; checking the mouth, which includes the gum color and signs of gum disease along with plaque buildup; checking the ears for signs of an infection or ear mites; examining the eyes; and, last but not least, checking the condition of the skin and coat. Next, she should discuss the proper diet and the quantity of food to give your puppy. If this is different from your breeder's recommendation, then you should see if she approves of the breeder's choice. It is also customary to take a small stool sample for a test for intestinal parasites. It must be fresh, preferably within 12 hours, since the eggs hatch quickly and after hatching they will not be observed under the microscope. If your pet won't oblige, usually the technician can take a sample in the clinic.

Puppy Health Care

Puppy Vaccination Schedule

8 weeks of age—Distemper, hepatitis, leptospirosis, parainfluenza, parvovirus (often given as a combination shot called DHLPP), and Lyme disease.

10 to 11 weeks—Distemper, hepatitis, leptospirosis, parainfluenza, parvovirus, and bordetella

13 to 15 weeks—Distemper, hepatitis, leptospirosis, parainfluenza, parvovirus, and Lyme disease

16 to 18 weeks—Rabies and bordetella

Immunizations

It is important that you take your puppy's vaccination record with you on your first visit. Presumably, the breeder has started the puppy on a vaccination schedule that is current up to the time that you acquired custody of the dog. Veterinarians differ in their vaccination protocol. It is not unusual for your puppy to have received vaccinations for distemper, hepatitis, leptospirosis, parvovirus, and parainfluenza every two to three weeks from the age of five or six weeks. This is usually a combined injection typically called the DHLPP.

Vaccine Concerns

Although there are potential problems with vaccines, it does not mean that you should not vaccinate your puppy. Modern vaccinations have saved an uncountable number of dogs from deadly diseases that would have caused them death in the past. If you are concerned about certain vaccinations or schedules, discuss them with your veterinarian and come to a solution that will be safe for your puppy's health.

Dogs can catch diseases from other dogs, so be sure that your puppy is fully vaccinated before taking him out to make friends.

Why are so many immunizations necessary? No one knows for sure when the puppy's maternal antibodies are gone, although it is customarily accepted that distemper antibodies are gone by 12 weeks. Usually parvovirus antibodies are gone by 16 to 18 weeks of age. However, it is possible for the maternal antibodies to be gone at a much earlier age or even a later age. Therefore immunizations are started at an early age. The vaccine will not give immunity as long as there are maternal antibodies.

Fleas

These pests are not only a dog's worst enemy, but are also an enemy to you, your house, your yard, and your pocketbook. Once fleas infiltrate the area where your puppy is, they can be very difficult to get rid of. Not only are they nuisances, but they are dangerous to the health of your puppy as well. Most dogs are allergic to the bite of a flea, and in many cases, it only takes one flea bite to start an allergic reaction, which usually results in open sores or flea bite dermatitis. A heavy infestation of these pests can cause blood loss and then anemia, which can be fatal to young, tiny pups. Preventing fleas is the key, not to mention less expensive in the long run.

Fortunately, there are several good products available today. If there is a flea infestation, no one product is going to correct the problem. Not only will the dog require treatment, so will the environment. However, some products are not usable on young puppies and treating fleas should be done under your veterinarian's guidance. There are systemic, topical products and pills available, such as Program, Advantage, and Sentinel. The topical products can be placed directly onto your dog's fur on his back near his shoulder blades, and the pills can be taken on a daily basis. Treat all pets in your household for fleas at the same time, because they are easily passed from one to the other.

Finding Fleas

If you aren't sure that your dog has fleas, have him lie down on a solid, light-colored sheet or blanket. Comb his coat thoroughly, especially around his stomach, in his "armpits," and around his tail (these out-of-the-way places are where fleas like to hide). After you have brushed him, let him up and check out the sheet. If there is any residue on the sheet, the brush, or the comb that looks like salt (which are flea eggs) and pepper (which are flea dirt or fecal matter), your dog has fleas.

Ticks

Ticks are known carriers of disease for both animals and humans— they carry Rocky Mountain Spotted Fever and Lyme disease and can cause tick paralysis. These eight-legged oval insects will bury their headparts in your puppy's skin and live off his blood. You can remove them with tweezers, and with a slow, twisting motion, by pulling out the head. Although using flea-preventive products can help repel some ticks, they are not totally effective. The best way to ensure that your dog doesn't have any is to examine him regularly, especially if he has been in a place where ticks like to hide, like wooded areas or tall brush.

Worms

Yuck! Yes, internal parasites are disgusting, and they can also be very dangerous for your puppy. They can be found in very young puppies, because many can be passed from mother to offspring, either while in the womb or through nursing. They are also dangerous because you actually can't see them, and many times, your puppy will not show any obvious symptoms until he is very ill. Intestinal parasites are more prevalent in some areas than others. Climate, soil, and contamination are big factors that contribute to the incidence of intestinal parasites.

How does your puppy get these things? A dog with worms may go to the bathroom in the local park. Parasite eggs are passed in the stool, lie on the ground, and then become infective in a certain number of days. Your puppy may sniff or lick at the feces or may get some on his fur or paws and lick it off. Your best chance of your puppy becoming and remaining worm-free is to always pooper-scoop your yard and watch your puppy in public places where other

Puppies can pick up parasites like fleas and ticks while playing outdoors. Be sure to check your pup's coat thoroughly.

Good grooming practices can help you keep on top of any parasites, such as fleas, ticks, or mites, which may affect your puppy's health.

dogs may be. Also, a fence helps to keep strange dogs out of your yard. Other good ways to avoid worms is to keep your puppy free of fleas, ticks, and other external parasites and to have him checked for worms regularly. Your veterinarian should perform a fecal examination on your dog twice a year or more often if there is a problem. Your dog should be checked for hookworms, roundworms, whipworms, tapeworms, coccidiosis,

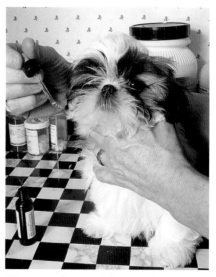

Worms can be passed from mother to puppy; all puppies should be checked and treated for internal parasites at their first veterinary checkup.

giardia, and heartworm disease. If your dog has a positive fecal sample, then he will be given the appropriate medication, and you will be asked to bring back another stool sample in a certain period of time (depending on the type of worm). Once he is all clear, he then will be rewormed. This process goes on until he has at least two negative samples. The different types of worms require different medications, so don't waste your money or your puppy's time buying over-the-counter medication without first consulting your veterinarian.

To ensure against genetic disease and to preserve the quality of their lines, responsible breeders will screen all of their puppies before breeding them.

Puppy Health Care

Your puppy will rely on you to keep him in good health.

Quick & Easy Puppy Care and Training

Spaying or Neutering

When you purchased a pet-quality puppy from a breeder or got your puppy from a shelter, it was probably requested that you have him or her neutered or spayed. Your breeder's or shelter's request is based on what is healthiest for your dog and what is most beneficial for your breed.

For purebred dogs, experienced and conscientious breeders devote many years into developing a bloodline. In order to do this, they make every effort to plan each breeding in regard to conformation, temperament, and health. This type of breeder does his best to perform the necessary testing (i.e., OFA, CERF, testing for inherited blood disorders, thyroid, etc.). Reputable breeders do not want their offspring to be bred indiscriminately. Of course there is always the exception, and your breeder may agree to let you breed your dog under his direct supervision. This is an important concept. More and more effort is being made to breed healthier dogs.

Keeping the Weight Off

Some people worry about their dog gaining weight after being neutered or spayed. This is usually not the case. Most dogs are just as active as they were before surgery. However, if your dog should begin to gain weight, then you need to decrease his food and see to it that he gets a little more exercise.

Shelters and humane societies make the request to neuter your puppy because they see firsthand the problems of pet overpopulation and wish to spare any resulting puppy of any litter the pain of being placed in a shelter.

Index

Photo Credits

Paulette Braun, p. 13
All other photographs by Isabelle Francais